Searchlight BOOKS™

Fake News

What Are

Conspiracy Theories?

Margaret J. Goldstein

Lerner Publications ◆ Minneapolis

Lerner Publications Company
An imprint of Lerner Publishing Group, Inc.
241 First Avenue North
Minneapolis, MN 55401 USA

For reading levels and more information, look up this title at www.lernerbooks.com.

Main body text set in Adrianna Regular.
Typeface provided by Chank.

Library of Congress Cataloging-in-Publication Data

Names: Goldstein, Margaret J., author.
Title: What are conspiracy theories? / Margaret J. Goldstein.
Description: Minneapolis : Lerner Publications, [2020] | Series: Searchlight
    books—Fake news | Audience: Ages: 8–11. | Audience: Grades: 4 to 6. | Includes
    bibliographical references and index.
Identifiers: LCCN 2018059342 (print) | LCCN 2019004885 (ebook) |
    ISBN 9781541556676 (eb pdf) | ISBN 9781541555778 (lib. bdg. : alk. paper) |
    ISBN 9781541574724 (pbk. : alk. paper)
Subjects: LCSH: Conspiracy theories—Juvenile literature.
Classification: LCC HV6275 (ebook) | LCC HV6275 .G53 2020 (print) |
    DDC 001.9—dc23

LC record available at https://lccn.loc.gov/2018059342

Manufactured in the United States of America
2-48925-43355-12/11/2019

Contents

PAGE PLUS+ Scan QR codes throughout for more content!

Chapter 1

LIES, PLOTS, AND SECRETS

In July 2019, Americans marked an important anniversary. Fifty years before, on July 20, 1969, US astronaut Neil

Armstrong became the first human to set foot on the moon. He and fellow astronaut Buzz Aldrin walked on the lunar (moon) surface, planted an American flag, and took pictures. Video cameras also recorded the event.

Buzz Aldrin walks on the lunar surface in 1969.

Thousands gather in front of giant TV screens in New York City to see humans set foot on the moon for the first time.

Back on Earth, viewers watched the moon landing on TV. They were awestruck. Humans had never before visited another body in space. They were witnessing history.

Enter the Skeptics

But not everyone celebrated. A few scientists, writers, and others had doubts. Flying humans to the moon was nearly impossible, they said. They had a few reasons why they thought so. On the way to the moon, spacecraft have to fly through a zone of powerful radiation. Doubters believed that this energy would have killed the astronauts.

Photos like this one from Armstrong and Aldrin's 1969 mission document their history-making feat—yet some still questioned whether the mission ever happened.

Famous news anchor Walter Cronkite holds an issue of the *New York Times* proclaiming that men landed on the moon.

Some photos and video from the moon also raised questions. The moon has no wind. But when the astronauts planted the American flag, it seemed to flutter in the breeze. The photos showed a starless sky too. If the photos were really taken on the moon, wouldn't they show millions of stars?

There was only one explanation, according to some: the 1969 moon landing and five more moon landings after it were faked, and Hollywood movie studios filmed them. But why fake the moon landings?

Photo evidence such as this picture of Buzz Aldrin on the moon wasn't enough to convince true skeptics.

At the time, the United States was competing with the Soviet Union (a former country that included modern-day Russia) to be the first and the best in space exploration. Putting astronauts on the moon would help the United States win this space race. But according to doubters, the US National Aeronautics and Space Administration (NASA) couldn't achieve its goal. So it faked the landings.

This NASA crew watches as Armstrong and Aldrin depart Earth for their mission to the moon.

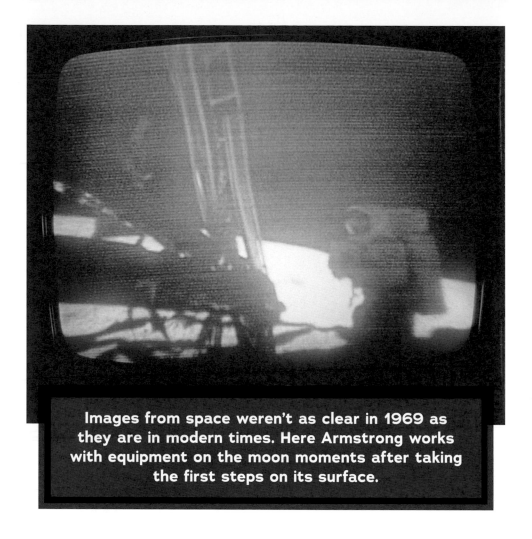

Images from space weren't as clear in 1969 as they are in modern times. Here Armstrong works with equipment on the moon moments after taking the first steps on its surface.

A Government Cover-Up!

Within ten years of the first moon landing, the idea that it was a hoax had grown into a full-blown conspiracy theory. A conspiracy theory is an explanation that involves a secret plot, a cover-up, or a shadowy network of powerful people behind the scenes. The explanation differs from the one given by government officials, reporters, and scientists.

Conspiracy theorists promoted the story of fake moon landings in books and films. Scientists explained why the theories were wrong. The American flag seemed to flutter, but only because the astronauts were adjusting its frame. The stars didn't show up in photos because of camera settings and glare from the sun. But to some, the explanations didn't matter. The conspiracy theory stuck.

Conspiracy theorists say that this very famous image was fabricated, or faked.

Chapter 2

SO MANY THEORIES!

Over the years, hundreds of conspiracy theories have developed. Some are more famous than others. After an assassin killed President John F. Kennedy in 1963, the US government investigated the crime. The investigation revealed that one man, acting alone, had murdered Kennedy. But conspiracy theorists had a different explanation. They said the US Central Intelligence Agency (CIA) had conspired with the Mafia, a powerful crime organization, to kill the president.

The *Birmingham Evening Mail* (UK) front page announces the news that Kennedy was shot.

Water vapor is the cause behind white streaks that trail airplanes, but some conspiracy theorists have doubts.

Another theory is about the streaky clouds trailing behind flying airplanes. Called contrails, these streaks are made of harmless water vapor. But in the late 1990s, a new conspiracy theory emerged. The streaks weren't harmless at all, some said. They contained poisonous chemicals. The government and the military released the chemicals from airplanes to sicken people on the ground below. The so-called chemtrails were part of an international conspiracy to control humans.

Believe It or Not

Like chemtrails and the Kennedy assassination, conspiracy theories spring out of real-world events and situations. Here are a few more:

In 1947, a military weather balloon crashed at a ranch in New Mexico. But according to conspiracy theorists, alien spacecraft crashed at the ranch. The US government was hiding the evidence.

Head intelligence officer Jesse Marcel investigated after a mysterious object crashed in New Mexico, and evidence showed it was a weather balloon.

Vaccines help the body fight diseases. But according to conspiracy theorists, vaccinations are harmful and drug companies promote and sell these dangerous substances to make millions of dollars.

Cities put fluoride in drinking water supplies to protect people from tooth decay. But according to conspiracy theorists, fluoride is poisonous. The government and big businesses put fluoride into water supplies to sicken citizens.

Shots may not be fun, but they protect against serious diseases such as measles and mumps.

What do all these conspiracy theories have in common? The conspirators are all big and powerful: governments, industry, and the military. They carry out their plots for power or money or as an excuse to go to war. And their control is said to be far-reaching. In many conspiracy theories, the villain is a secret international society.

When terrorists crashed a plane into the Pentagon on September 11, 2001, some conspiracy theorists said the US government was really behind the attack.

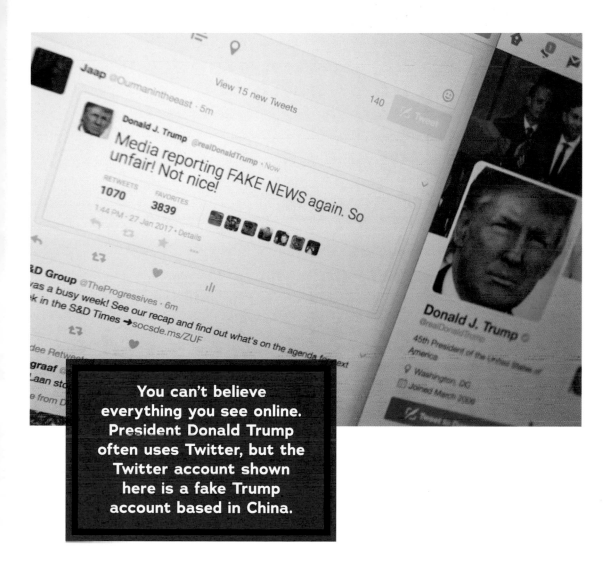

You can't believe everything you see online. President Donald Trump often uses Twitter, but the Twitter account shown here is a fake Trump account based in China.

Before the internet, conspiracy theories spread slowly. People learned about them through books, articles, and films. In the twenty-first century, conspiracy theories spread like wildfire. They spring up overnight and go viral on social media, sometimes even as real events are unfolding.

Real or Fake?

Is this story real or fake? See the Fake News Toolkit on page 29 to help you decide.

Kayla Hutchens
@Kayla_Hutchens

#Throwbackthursday is a government scheme. The National Security Agency puts old photos in databases to spy on us with facial recognition software. DELETE YOUR OLD PICTURES! #tbt

9:00 PM - July 17, 2019

 1   1   1

Fake! In posts like this one, the writer doesn't provide any sources or evidence for the information. If you type "Throwback Thursday," "National Security Agency," and "conspiracy theory" into a search engine, you'll find this misinformation on lists of conspiracy theories.

Scan the QR code to try another example.

Chapter 3

WHO'S FALLING FOR THE THEORIES?

Why do people believe conspiracy theories? Some distrust the government, the military, or big business. Others are searching for simple answers to difficult problems. For example, most scientists agree that humans have caused global climate change by burning large amounts of coal, oil, and natural gas. Burning these fuels adds heat-trapping gases to the air. So Earth is getting hotter.

Coal plants like this one contribute to global climate change.

But some Americans don't believe the scientists. They think climate change is a conspiracy cooked up by environmentalists and scientists. Why? To boost their careers and to get money for their studies. Conspiracy theorists say that scientists falsify studies and statistics to show that Earth is getting hotter. For some people, it's easier to believe in the conspiracy than to face the fact that Earth is warming. They don't want to believe that Earth may get too hot for humans, plants, and animals in the future.

Melting glaciers are one result of global climate change.

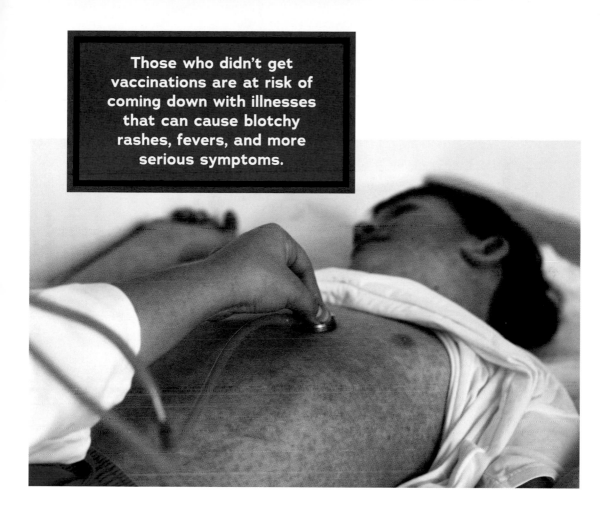

Those who didn't get vaccinations are at risk of coming down with illnesses that can cause blotchy rashes, fevers, and more serious symptoms.

Truth and Consequences

Some conspiracy theories are harmless. Believing that the US government is hiding aliens in New Mexico probably won't hurt anyone. But other conspiracy theories are dangerous. Those who think vaccines are part of a drug company plot might refuse vaccinations for their children. Without vaccines, the children might get sick and spread deadly diseases to others.

Conspiracy theorists have made false accusations against Muslims.

Some conspiracy theories make false claims about certain religious and ethnic groups. For example, some believe that Muslims (people who practice the Islamic religion) are part of a secret plot to replace US law with Islamic law. This false and ill-informed idea has appeared on social media and websites. It has led to hostility toward American Muslims. This kind of bias against different cultures is not new. It has happened throughout US history. For example, Irish and German immigrants used to be discriminated against.

Real or Fake?

Is this story real or fake? See the Fake News Toolkit on page 29 to help you decide.

DAILY NEWS

No. 49,725 | THE BEST SELLING NEWSPAPER IN THE WORLD | Today's Edition

National - World - Business - Lifestyle - Travel - Technology - Sport - Weather

The CIA's Strange Attempt on a Life

Everyone knows Fidel Castro, leader of Cuba from 1959 to 2008, loved cigars. This fact led to a strange assassination attempt. The CIA put poison inside a box of Castro's favorite kind of cigars. But the cigars never made it to Castro's mouth. So the attempt failed.

View from the top

Lorem ipsum dolor sit amet, Consectetur adipiscing elit. Vivamus sit amet odio id lorem blandit luctus. Vivamus placerat viverra lorem. Vestibulum consectetur nunc vel sem luoreet dignissim. Cum sociis natoque penatibus et magnis dis parturient montes.

Consectetur adipiscing elit. Vi-

The best way to get something done is to begin

Donec sed turpis ligula. Vestibulum vitae dignissim eros, quis scelerisque lectus. Donec blandit

"Morbi lobortis lacinia, elit in suspendisse egestis, ullamcorper ligula erat,

Economy

Vivamus est elit, tristique id sollicitudin id, mattis et dolor. Morbi lobortis lacinia elit in euismod.

True! If you google "Fidel Castro poison cigar," you will find reports of the assassination plot from other reliable sources, such as CNN and several British newspapers.

Scan the QR code to try another example.

Chapter 4

FACT OR FICTION?

Conspiracy theories are not hard to find. The internet is full of them. Type "moon landing hoax" into a search engine, and read all about it. Visit Amazon.com and search for "chemtrails." You'll find dozens of books. Go to YouTube and search for "fluoride conspiracy." You'll find documentary films, with people claiming to be experts on fluoride, health, and the sinister plot to poison our drinking water.

Read what you see online with a critical eye!

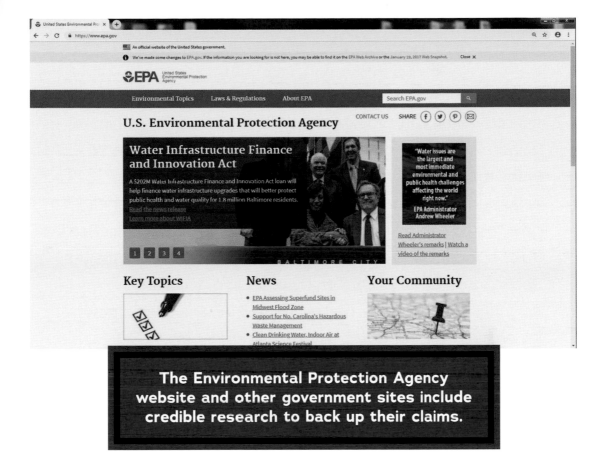

The Environmental Protection Agency website and other government sites include credible research to back up their claims.

At first, some arguments may seem to be well researched. They might include statistics and refer to scientific studies. But dig deeper. Does an article or film refer to "well-known scientists" without naming the scientists? Does an article include statistics without saying what organization gathered them? Does a website or film look sloppy and poorly made? Is it a website or source you've never heard of before? These are all clues that the information is not to be trusted.

Debunk Those Theories

If you doubt a conspiracy theory, do another internet search. After you type in "moon landing hoax," type in "moon landing hoax debunked." You'll find just as many websites that poke holes in the conspiracy theorists' arguments. Rational Wiki and Skeptic.com are websites devoted to debunking conspiracy theories, pseudoscience (fake science), and fake news. Some government websites debunk conspiracy theories by providing accurate scientific explanations. For example, NASA explains how jet engines create vapor trails.

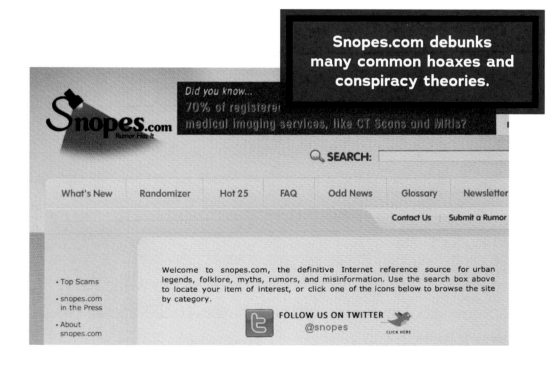

Snopes.com debunks many common hoaxes and conspiracy theories.

If you're searching for information, think about which sources you'd use to do research for school. Sources backed by scientists, doctors, and other experts are good places to start.

The best way to fight conspiracy theories is to use your head. For example, it would have taken hundreds of prop builders, special effects artists, and camera operators to create six fake moon landings in movie studios. Have all those people really been keeping the secret for fifty years? If the moon landings were really a hoax, wouldn't some of the film crew have spilled the beans by now?

Real or Fake?

Is this story real or fake? See the Fake News Toolkit on page 29 to help you decide.

Ryan Perez
@Ryan_Perez

I just heard from a friend in publishing that J. K. Rowling isn't a real person. She's made up!! Truth. A team of writers and advertisers created ALL of the Harry Potter books!! It was a big moneymaking scheme. The woman who poses as J. K. Rowling is an ACTOR they hired!! Mind. Blown. #harrypotter #jkrowling #jkrowlingisfake.

3:00 PM - Aug 1, 2019

 10   0   0

False! Posts like this one are suspicious. The writer says the information came from a "friend in publishing" but doesn't say who the friend is. The post doesn't link to articles from well-known news organizations. If you type "J. K. Rowling doesn't exist" into a search engine, you'll find this misinformation on a list of conspiracy theories.

Scan the QR code to try another example.

Fake News Toolkit

When you watch or read a news story, it can be difficult to spot fake news. People want you to believe what they believe. Many try hard to convince you, even if they have to lie or twist facts. Read on to arm yourself with some tools for spotting fake news.

Consider the Source

Does the news come from a respected media source? News items that come from little-known sources are more likely to be fake. Learn about the organization that published the story. Is its purpose to provide fair, objective news?

Look for Objectivity

If an article tells only one side of a story, it might be fake news. A good news story should look at an issue from all sides and let readers come to their own conclusions.

Check the Facts

Don't just accept any information that a news story gives you. Follow up. Find out where the information comes from. Do the figures and surprising facts presented come with sources? And if they do, can you follow up on them?

Don't Spread It

If you see a story that you think might be fake news, don't spread it! Don't like it or share it. Don't even click on it. The best way to make fake news go away is to ignore it.

Report It

Google, Facebook, and many other websites now have buttons that allow you to report fake news. If you are sure an item is fake, report it. That can help stop the spread of the story and prevent it from fooling others.

Glossary

conspiracy theory: an explanation for an event or situation that involves a secret plot carried out by powerful individuals or organizations

conspirator: a person who schemes or makes plots as part of a group

conspire: to join in a secret agreement to commit a wrongful act

cover-up: a systemic effort to keep a crime or misdeed from being known to the public

debunk: to expose something as a fake or hoax

evidence: something that provides proof, such as a photograph, official document, or eyewitness report

fake news: news items or social media posts that are mostly or wholly untrue but are designed to look like real news stories

plot: a secret plan, usually made to accomplish an evil or criminal deed

pseudoscience: theories, beliefs, and practices that are said to be based on science but that actually have no scientific foundation

statistics: a collection of data gathered using scientific methods

Learn More about Conspiracy Theories

Books

Corso, Phil. *Conspiracy Theories and Fake News.* New York: PowerKids, 2018. Conspiracy theories are part of a larger trend called fake news. This book helps readers figure out how to spot the fakes and separate fact from fiction.

Jeffries, Joyce. *What's Fake News?* New York: KidHaven, 2019. This title explores how fake news affects our politics and society.

Lindeen, Mary. *Smart Internet Surfing: Evaluating Websites and Advertising.* Minneapolis: Lerner Publications, 2016. Just because you see something online doesn't make it true. This book helps you evaluate whether an internet site is trustworthy or not.

Websites

Junior Skeptic
https://www.skeptic.com/junior_skeptic/
The Skeptics Society offers articles and books just for kids. This website gives more information about the society and its publications.

Media Smarts
https://mediasmarts.ca
On this website from Canada's Centre for Digital and Media Literacy, kids can play interactive games to learn about fake news, online advertising, online privacy, cybersecurity, and more.

Safe Search Kids
https://www.safesearchkids.com
This website offers tips to help kids navigate the internet safely and responsibly.

Index

Photo Acknowledgments

Image credits: NASA, pp. 4, 6, 8, 9, 11; AP Photo, p. 5; CBS Photo Archive/Getty Images, p. 7; Bettmann/Getty Images, p. 10; Mirrorpix/Getty Images, p. 12; Isannes/E+/Getty Images, p. 13; Universal History Archive/UIG/Getty Images, p. 14; JPC-PROD/Shutterstock.com, p. 15; Alex Wong/ Getty Images, p. 16; Jaap Arriens/NurPhoto/Getty Images, p. 17; fonikum/DigitalVision Vectors/ Getty Images, pp. 18, 28 (profile photo); acilo/iStock/Getty Images, p. 19; MB Photography/ Moment/Getty Images, p. 20; fotohay/Shutterstock.com, p. 21; pandapix/iStock Editorial/Getty Images, p. 22; bgblue/DigitalVision Vectors/Getty Images, p. 23; Ridofranzagency/iStock/Getty Images, p. 24; US Environmental Protection Agency, p. 25; NetPhotos/Alamy Stock Photo, p. 26; Monkey Business Images/Getty Images, p. 27.

Cover: Richard B. Levine/Alamy Stock Photo (newspapers); National Archives (documents).